Learn
How to Count
Money
Quickly
United States
Penny, Nickel, Dime, Quarter, Half, Dollar

2nd Grade Level
Counting Book

Copyright © 2018 Victor Scott Adcock

Bold New Life Publishing, LLC

boldnewlife.com

ISBN 13:978-1-947280-12-0
ISBN 10:1-947280-12-0

One Dollar is the same as 100 pennies.

One Dollar is the same as one hundred pennies.

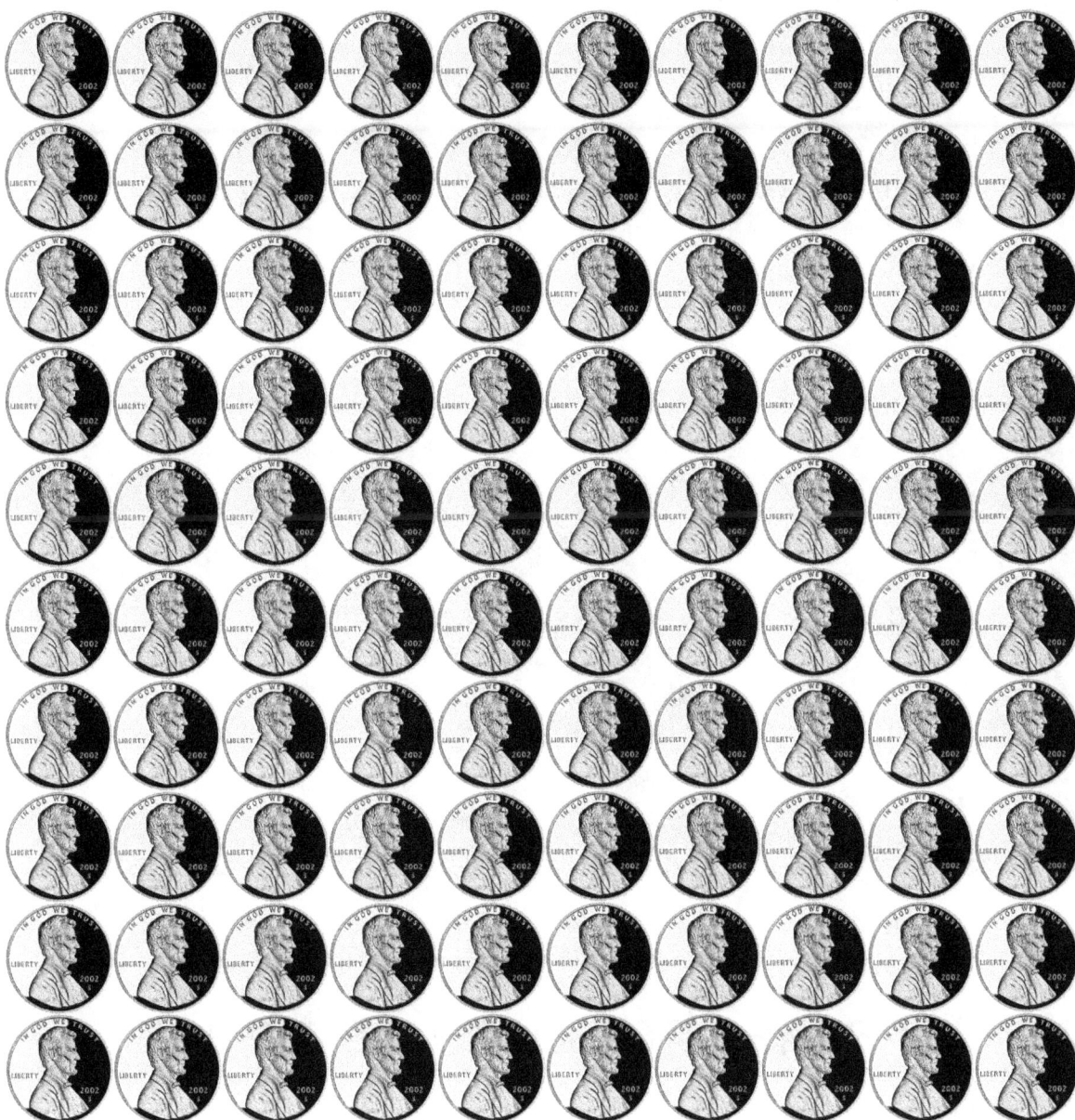

100 Pennies

Pennies have a smooth edge and brownish or copper color.

One Dollar is the same as 20 nickels.

One Dollar is the same as twenty nickels.

Twenty nickels.

Remember nickels have a smooth edge.

One nickel is worth 5 pennies

It is easy to count nickels by fives.

5, 10, 15, 20, 25, 30, 35, 40, 45, 50, 55, 60, 65, 70, 75, 80, 85, 90, 95, 100.   Or One Dollar 1.00

Remember, 20 nickels is the same as 1.00   One Dollar

Dollars are before the . period
Cents are after the . period or dot.

One Dollar is the same as 10 dimes.

There are grooves on the edge of a dime

Ten Dimes are worth the same as 100 pennies.

The dime is the smallest and thinnest of all United States coins. One dime is worth ten pennies.

You can count Dimes by tens.

10, 20, 30, 40, 50, 60, 70, 80, 90,100 or 1.00 One Dollar.

Remember 10 dimes is equal to 1 dollar.

	10		60
	20		70
	30		80
	40		90
	50		1.00

One Dollar is the same as 4 quarters.

There are grooves in the edge of a quarter.

Four quarters is the same amount of money as a one dollar bill.

Count quarters by 25s

25

50

75

100

One Dollar is the same as 2 half dollar coins.

One Dollar is the same as two half dollar coins.

The half dollar coin is much larger than the quarter. These coins are still available from the bank but not used very often.

1 half dollar coin is the same as 50 pennies.

It is easier to start with the largest value coin first when counting a mixture of change.

Value of each coin.   Total

.25   25

.10   35

.10   45

.05   50

.01   51

Value		Total

.25		25

.05		30

.01		31

.01		32

.01		33

Value		Total
.10		10
.10		20
.10		30
.05		35
.05		40
.01		41
.01		42

Value		Total
.05		05
.05		10
.05		15
.05		20
.01		21
.01		22
.01		23 cents

Value		Total

.25		25

.25		50

.10		60

.10		70

.05		75

.75

Great job
Keep practicing at home with
Real money.

Value		Total
.10		10
.05		15
.05		20
.01		21
.01		22

.22 cents

Value		Total

.25 _____

.10 _____

.10 _____

.05 _____

.05 _____

.01 _____

Value	Total

___._____   _____

___._____   _____

___._____   _____

___._____   _____

___._____   _____

You can do this!

There's always a better way to teach and there's always something to learn.

Multiplication Books

For Beginners

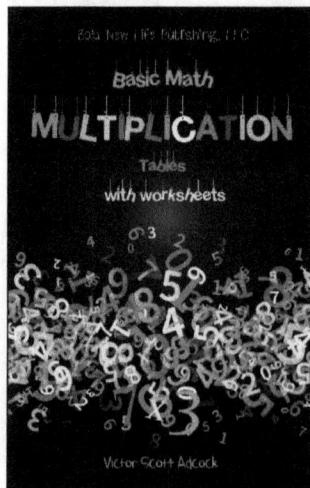

3rd and 4th Grade Level

Bold New Life Publishing, LLC

There's always a better way to teach and
There's always something to learn.

Victor Scott Adcock

Copyright © 2018 Victor Scott Adcock

Bold New Life Publishing, LLC

boldnewlife.com

All rights reserved.

ISBN 13:978-1-947280-12-0
ISBN 10:1-947280-12-0